Dear Future Me

A Journal to Level Up Your Life

Dr. Marlon Fuller

Copyright © 2025

Copyright © 2025 by Dr. Marlon Fuller
All rights reserved.

No part of this publication may be reproduced, stored in a retrieval system, or transmitted in any form or by any means—electronic, mechanical, photocopying, recording, or otherwise—without prior written permission from the publisher, except in the case of brief quotations embodied in critical articles or reviews.

This journal is a work of original content designed for personal development and reflection. While the prompts and challenges are inspired by real-life scenarios, any resemblance to actual persons, living or dead, is purely coincidental unless otherwise stated.

For information, permissions, or bulk orders, please contact:
info@coolkids.org
or visit www.coolkids.org

Printed in the United States of America.
ISBN: 979-8-9899421-4-5

First Edition
Cover and interior design by Samarpita Banerjee

CONTENTS

FOREWORD 05

Chapter 1: PASSION 06

Chapter 2: PURPOSE 12

Chapter 3: POTENTIAL 18

Chapter 4: CONFIDENCE 24

Chapter 5: GRATITUDE 30

Chapter 6: COURAGE 36

Chapter 7: PATIENCE 42

Chapter 8: DETERMINATION 48

Chapter 9: SELF-LOVE 54

Chapter 10: MINDFULNESS 60

Chapter 11: KINDNESS 66

Chapter 12: EMPOWERMENT 72

Chapter 13: SELF-DISCIPLINE 78

Chapter 14: OPTIMISM 84

Chapter 15: FOCUS 90

Chapter 16: RESILIENCE 96

Chapter 17: LEADERSHIP 102

Chapter 18: INTEGRITY 108

Chapter 19: BALANCE 114

Chapter 20: HUMILITY 120

Chapter 21: CHANGE 126

Chapter 22: SUCCESS 132

Chapter 23: LEGACY 138

Chapter 24: PROSPERITY 144

ABOUT THE AUTHOR 150

FOREWORD

Over the years, I've had the privilege of working with thousands of students, educators, and families. What's stayed with me most isn't the test scores or the graduation rates. It's the moments when a student discovers who they are and begins to imagine who they can become. That's the real heart of education.

Dear Future Me: A Journal to Level Up Your Life is a tool that helps students do just that. It's thoughtful, relatable, and built with a clear understanding of what young people need today, not just academically but emotionally and personally. It encourages students to pause, reflect, set goals, and take meaningful steps toward the future they want to create.

What I appreciate most about this journal is how flexible it is. It works just as well in a classroom as it does in a counseling office or at the kitchen table. It invites students to take ownership of their story while also giving parents and educators a way to support and guide them along the way.

This isn't just another workbook. It's a conversation starter. It's a mirror and a map. And it's written with real heart. It's a powerful resource that reflects what education should always strive to do: prepare young people not just for the next test but for the rest of their lives.

DR. CHARLES WARNER
FORMER SUPERINTENDENT
NEW HAVEN PUBLIC SCHOOLS

CHAPTER 1

Passion
IGNITING THE FIRE THAT FUELS YOU

"Passion is energy. Feel the power that comes from focusing on what excites you."

— Oprah Winfrey

School wasn't his idea of a good time, but when Jordan was introduced to the school's music program, things began to change. It was different: he couldn't imagine spending more than 30 minutes on a math problem, but he would happily spend hours in the music room, tweaking mixes and experimenting with instrumentals. When his teacher commented on how much more alive he looked when playing music, Jordan realized that it wasn't just a subject – it was a passion.

You see, passion doesn't always announce itself with fireworks. Sometimes it shows up quietly, like curiosity or excitement. In this case, Jordan had no idea he would enjoy music; he only discovered his passion once he began to experiment. Passion often reveals itself when we're exploring, trying, and creating. The goal isn't to find it instantly — It's to keep an open mind and let it discover you.

Journal Prompts

- What's something you love doing, even if no one's watching?

- When was the last time you felt excited about learning something new?

- What would your perfect afternoon look like if you could do anything?

Challenge of the Week:

Spend 15 minutes this week doing something you enjoy just because. No grades. No audience. Just you and your spark.

Mindset Reminder:

"My passion is a compass. I can trust where it leads."

CHAPTER 2

Purpose
DISCOVERING YOUR WHY

"The two most important days in your life are the day you are born and the day you find out why."
— Mark Twain

Community service is easy credit, and Leila needed the boost. She volunteered at a local community food pantry, thinking that she'd get in, pack a few shelves, and get out. But when she handed a lunch pack to a little girl who whispered "thank you" as though she'd just received the greatest gift ever, something changed inside Leila. To her surprise, she found that she enjoyed her time at the pantry and volunteered regularly – easy extra credit, but because it felt right. Her why became clear: she wanted to build a life where she could keep showing up for others.

Purpose isn't about a job title, it's about impact. Leila discovered hers by doing something small and meaningful. Your purpose often begins with paying attention to what moves you. It lives at the intersection of what you care about and what the world needs.

Journal Prompts

- What kinds of moments make you feel proud, even when no one notices?

- What problem do you wish you could help solve in the world?

- Who inspires you, and why?

Challenge of the Week:

Do one thing this week that helps someone else, no spotlight needed.

Mindset Reminder:

"My life has purpose, and I'm discovering it one step at a time."

CHAPTER 3

Potential

UNLOCKING WHAT'S ALREADY INSIDE

"There is no heavier burden than an untapped potential."
— *Charles Schulz*

Every class has a quiet kid, the kind who never speaks up, never socializes, never even asks to go to the bathroom. That was Tony. But while he hardly ever spoke out loud, he nevertheless had a way with words that most people never got the chance to see — until the talent show, that is. Tony got up on stage and recited a slam poem he had written about his absent father. The room fell silent at once, then erupted into applause. It was a response he never expected, but it was just the one he needed.

And for the first time in his life, Tony felt as though his potential had finally been recognized.

Your potential isn't something you have to earn. It's already in you, waiting to be expressed. Sometimes all it takes is one opportunity, one risk, one step forward to unlock it. You don't need to be loud to be powerful. You just need to be real.

Journal Prompts

- What's something you've done that surprised even you?

- What's one gift or talent you haven't shared yet? Why not?

- If fear wasn't a factor, what would you try tomorrow?

Challenge of the Week:

Take a small risk this week. Speak up. Share your work. Apply. Step into your strength.

CHAPTER 4

Confidence
BELIEVING IN YOURSELF

"Believe you can and you're halfway there."

— Theodore Roosevelt

Still waters run deep, and Eli's were a whirlpool in a trench. His journals and sketchbooks were filled with drawings, detailed pieces that he guarded like some forbidden secret. When his art teacher noticed them while peeking over his shoulder one day, she encouraged Eli to show them to the class. Overcome with dread, he nervously revealed the drawings, expecting to be mocked and criticized. To his surprise, everyone was amazed, and he couldn't believe that he had let fear rule his life for so long.

Confidence isn't about being perfect or always knowing what to do. It's about trusting yourself enough to take risks and be vulnerable. The more you believe in your worth, the more others will too. Confidence builds through action and self-acceptance.

Journal Prompts

- What's one thing you've accomplished that made you proud?

- When do you feel most confident?

- What's a small step you can take to boost your confidence this week?

Challenge of the Week:

Try something that scares you, even if it's just something small. Take a step outside your comfort zone.

Mindset Reminder:

"I am worthy. I am capable. I am confident."

CHAPTER 5

Gratitude

FINDING JOY IN EVERY MOMENT

"Gratitude turns what we have into enough."

— Melody Beattie

Carlos couldn't think of any better way to spend the holidays than playing video games and watching Netflix, so when the power unexpectedly went out, he felt cheated and outraged. Now forced to spend time with his family, it was his grandmother who reminded him that there were still plenty of things to be grateful for, things that he had which others did not. Over a warm cup of tea, Carlos and his grandmother took in the night sky; without any streetlights, the stars shone bright, and Carlos remembered that there were still plenty of things to enjoy about life.

Gratitude is a powerful tool that changes the way you see the world. It's not about ignoring the hard stuff, but about acknowledging the good, even in tough situations. By focusing on what you have, rather than what you don't, you can find joy in any moment.

Journal Prompts

- What are three things you're thankful for today?

- When was the last time you felt truly grateful?

- How can you express gratitude to someone this week?

Challenge of the Week:

Each day, write down one thing you're grateful for, no matter how small.

CHAPTER 6

Courage
DOING WHAT SCARES YOU

"Courage is not the absence of fear, but the triumph over it."

— Nelson Mandela

Olivia knew all the lines and memorized all the beats, but when it came time to audition for the school play, she was overcome with fear. Closing her eyes, she thought back to what her sister had told her. "Can a person be brave if they're afraid," Olivia had asked. "That is the only time a person can be brave," her sister answered. Swallowing hard, Olivia stepped into the audition room and gave it her all, and though she didn't get the part she wanted, she was glad that she tried.

Courage isn't the absence of fear; it's acting in spite of the fear. Everyone feels scared at times, but courage is about taking that step anyway. Every time you face your fears, you grow stronger, and the things that once seemed impossible become possible.

Journal Prompts

- What's something that scares you but excites you at the same time?

- When was the last time you felt courageous?

- How can you face one of your fears this week?

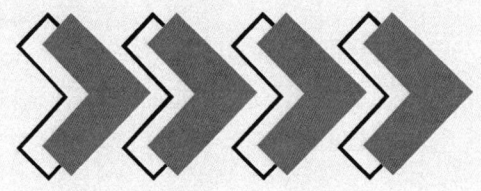

Challenge of the Week:

Choose one fear to face this week, big or small. Let courage lead the way.

Mindset Reminder:

"Courage doesn't mean fearlessness, it means acting in spite of fear."

CHAPTER 7

Patience
TRUSTING THE PROCESS

"Patience is not the ability to wait, but the ability to keep a good attitude while waiting."

— *Joyce Meyer*

Skateboarding didn't come as easily for Amir as it did for the other guys. When he just started, he could hardly balance, and things were slow going from there. The other guys slowly began to give up on him, viewing him as a lost cause. But Amir wouldn't have it. Though he had to work harder than everyone else, he set small goals for himself, improving slowly but surely. Eventually, he pulled off a trick he thought he would never be capable of, and he knew in that moment that all his hard work and patience had paid off.

Patience isn't just about waiting for something to happen. It's about staying positive and persistent, even when progress feels slow. Trusting the process helps you stay focused, even when the results don't show up right away.

Journal Prompts

- What's something you've been working on that requires patience?

- How do you keep a positive attitude when things aren't going as planned?

- When have you seen patience bring you success?

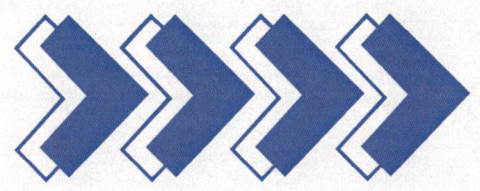

Challenge of the Week:

Practice patience in one area of your life this week, whether it's school, relationships, or a hobby.

Mindset Reminder:

"Patience is power. It's about trusting the journey, even when it's slow."

CHAPTER 8

Determination
STAYING FOCUSED ON YOUR GOALS

"The difference between who you are and who you want to be is what you do."

— *Unknown*

Hannah knew she wanted to be a professional dancer, but as far as career goals went, it wasn't as if the path had been neatly laid out in front of her. Nevertheless, she showed up to every class, practiced for hours on end, and worked through every obstacle that was thrown her way. She was determined to improve, and – finally, after years of hard work, she earned a scholarship to a prestigious dance academy.

REFLECTION:

Determination is the fuel that keeps you moving, even when things get tough. It's not about doing everything perfectly. It's about pushing through challenges and staying committed to your goals, even when you don't see immediate results.

Journal Prompts

- What's one goal you're determined to achieve?

- When did you feel like giving up, but kept going anyway?

- How do you stay motivated when progress feels slow?

Challenge of the Week:

Identify one goal you've been putting off and take one action toward it this week.

Mindset Reminder:

"Determination is my superpower. I can achieve anything I set my mind to."

CHAPTER 9

Self-Love

EMBRACING YOUR UNIQUENESS

"You yourself, as much as anybody in the entire universe, deserve your love and affection."

—*Buddha*

In the cutthroat world of high school society, comparing yourself to others is hard to avoid, and Sophie felt like she kept coming up short. One day, her mom told her, "True beauty comes from within, and when you love yourself, others will see that light." Though she had previously tried to change things about her appearance and personality to fit in, Sophie started practicing self-love by writing down things she liked about herself each day. Slowly, she began to feel more confident and embraced the very things about herself that her younger self would have wanted to change.

Self-love is the foundation of all other types of love. When you appreciate who you are, flaws and all, you give yourself the space to grow. Loving yourself isn't about being perfect, it's about accepting yourself as you are and knowing that you are enough.

Journal Prompts

- What are five things you love about yourself?

- How can you show yourself love today?

- When was the last time you felt truly at peace with who you are?

Challenge of the Week:

Practice one act of self-care every day this week, whether it's taking a break, going for a walk, or saying something kind to yourself.

Mindset Reminder:

"I am worthy of love, and I choose to love myself fully."

CHAPTER 10

Mindfulness
LIVING IN THE PRESENT MOMENT

"Mindfulness isn't difficult. We just need to remember to do it."

— Sharon Salzberg

Wherever he went and whatever he did, Ethan always looked like he was in a hurry. One day, he came across mindfulness meditation and, wanting a break from all the stress, decided to give it a try. At first, he felt silly, but as he practiced being present, he started to notice small details he'd never paid attention to before. His world became brighter and calmer. Mindfulness taught him to appreciate the moment instead of always thinking about what's next.

Mindfulness is about focusing on the present, and learning to let go of the past without worrying about the future. By being fully present in each moment, you can experience life more fully. It's in the little things, like a sunset, a smile, a quiet moment, that you find peace.

Journal Prompts

- What helps you stay in the present moment?

- When was the last time you felt completely at peace?

- How can you incorporate mindfulness into your daily routine?

Challenge of the Week:

Practice mindfulness for five minutes each day this week, focusing on your breath, surroundings, or a simple activity.

Mindset Reminder:

"I am fully present in this moment, and I embrace the peace it brings."

CHAPTER 11

Kindness
SPREADING POSITIVITY

"No act of kindness, no matter how small, is ever wasted."

— Aesop

Lily was what you might call a "gentle soul". She was effortlessly kind, and when she saw one of her classmates sitting alone at lunch, she came to sit with him to keep him company. It was a simple thing but it sparked a friendship that lasted all throughout their high school years. Looking back, it was all the proof she needed that kindness – even the small acts – can have a big impact.

Kindness is a superpower. It's a small act that can have a ripple effect, touching people in ways you may never know. Being kind not only helps others but also nurtures your own happiness and sense of belonging.

Journal Prompts

- How do you feel when someone is kind to you?

- What's one kind act you can do for someone this week?

- How can kindness make a difference in your community?

Mindset Reminder:

"Kindness is my strength. The more I give, the more I receive."

CHAPTER 12

Empowerment
TAKING CONTROL OF YOUR LIFE

"The most common way people give up their power is by thinking they don't have any."

— Alice Walker

Sarah was always quick to blame her circumstances for the things that went wrong in her life. It took her being given a leadership role in her school's volunteer program to see things differently. All of a sudden, she felt more empowered and more capable of enacting changes of her own. By stepping into her own power, Sarah began to make decisions that helped her grow, not just as a leader, but as a person.

Empowerment comes from understanding your own worth and abilities. When you take control of your actions and choices, you create the life you want. Empowerment isn't about domination; it's about embracing your strengths and using them to shape your future.

Journal Prompts

- What's one area of your life where you can take more control?

- When did you feel the most empowered?

- What's one thing you can do this week to feel more in control?

Challenge of the Week:

Identify one goal and take the first step toward achieving it this week.

Mindset Reminder:

"I am in charge of my destiny. I have the power to create the life I want."

Chapter 13

Self-Discipline
STAYING COMMITTED TO YOUR GOALS

"Success is the sum of small efforts, repeated day in and day out."
— Robert Collier

Jade wanted to be a writer, and she knew she had the talent and skill to make it happen. What she didn't have was self-discipline, however, and she found herself procrastinating day in and day out. She would normally blame it on writer's block, but the novelty of this excuse wore off quickly. Instead, she decided to create a writing schedule, even if it meant writing just 500 words a day. At first, it felt like the most difficult thing in the world, but over time, it became a habit. After a few months, she had a completed manuscript. Jade learned that self-discipline wasn't about doing everything at once. It was about taking consistent, small steps.

Self-discipline is the ability to stay focused on your goals, even when distractions arise. It's about showing up every day, even when you don't feel like it. The more you practice self-discipline, the easier it becomes to achieve the things that matter most.

Journal Prompts

- What's one goal you've struggled to stay committed to?

- How do you stay disciplined when you feel distracted or unmotivated?

- What's one small step you can take today to move closer to your goal?

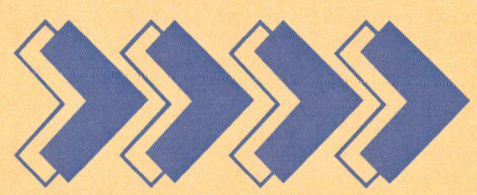

Challenge of the Week:

Create a simple, actionable plan for a goal and stick to it for the entire week.

Mindset Reminder:

"Discipline leads to freedom. Each small step brings me closer to my dreams."

CHAPTER 14

Optimism
SEEING THE BRIGHT SIDE

"A pessimist sees the difficulty in every opportunity; an optimist sees the opportunity in every difficulty."

— *Winston Churchill*

Moving to a new city and going to a different school comes with plenty of challenges, a fact Tommy was keenly aware of. At first, he was frustrated - everything was so different, and he felt like a fish out of water.. But his grandmother imparted some age-old folk wisdom on him. "When life gives you lemons, make lemonade," she said. It was a saying he'd heard before, but it was only then that Tommy started looking for the positive in every situation. His perspective shifted, and he began to enjoy the new experiences his move had brought.

Optimism is about focusing on the good, even when things seem tough. It doesn't mean ignoring problems; it means choosing to see challenges as opportunities for growth. The more you practice optimism, the easier it becomes to find the silver lining in any situation.

Journal Prompts

- What's one difficult situation you've experienced that turned out better than expected?

- How do you stay optimistic when things don't go as planned?

- What's one thing you can do today to focus on the positive?

Challenge of the Week:

Each day this week, find one positive thing in every situation, even if it's small.

Mindset Reminder:

"I choose to see the good in every situation, and I remain hopeful for the future."

CHAPTER 15

Focus

KEEPING YOUR EYE ON THE PRIZE

"The successful warrior is the average man, with laser-like focus."

— *Bruce Lee*

Kiana had had enough of her parents and elders telling her that she was always on her phone. How could that be true, she wondered, if I always do my homework? But the more she thought about it, the more she realized how easily distracted she was. To prove her parents wrong, Kiana set aside just 30 minutes per day for work, and found a quiet spot free from distractions. Her productivity improved within a week, and looking back she realized: it was the phone.

Focus is about narrowing your attention to what truly matters. When you give your full attention to one task at a time, you accomplish more and reduce stress. Focus helps you avoid distractions and stay on track toward your goals.

Journal Prompts

- What distracts you most often when you're trying to focus?

- How do you feel when you're focused on something important?

- What's one strategy you can use to improve your focus this week?

Challenge of the Week:

Pick one task and commit to focusing on it for at least 30 minutes without distractions.

Mindset Reminder:

"Focus brings clarity. By giving my full attention to the present moment. I unlock my potential."

CHAPTER 16

Resilience

BOUNCING BACK FROM SETBACKS

"It's not how hard you get hit, but how hard you can get hit and keep moving forward."

— Rocky Balboa

Just because you're passionate about something doesn't necessarily mean you're going to be good at it all the time. Maya learned this the hard way. She loved basketball, but her team suffered a run of bad losses that Maya couldn't help but feel responsible for. Though she could have thrown in the towel then and there, she decided to channel her frustrations into her training. Come next year, she was the best player on the team. Maya learned that setbacks are just setups for comebacks.

Resilience is the ability to keep going, even when things get tough. It's about bouncing back after failures and learning from them. When you develop resilience, you become stronger and more prepared for future challenges.

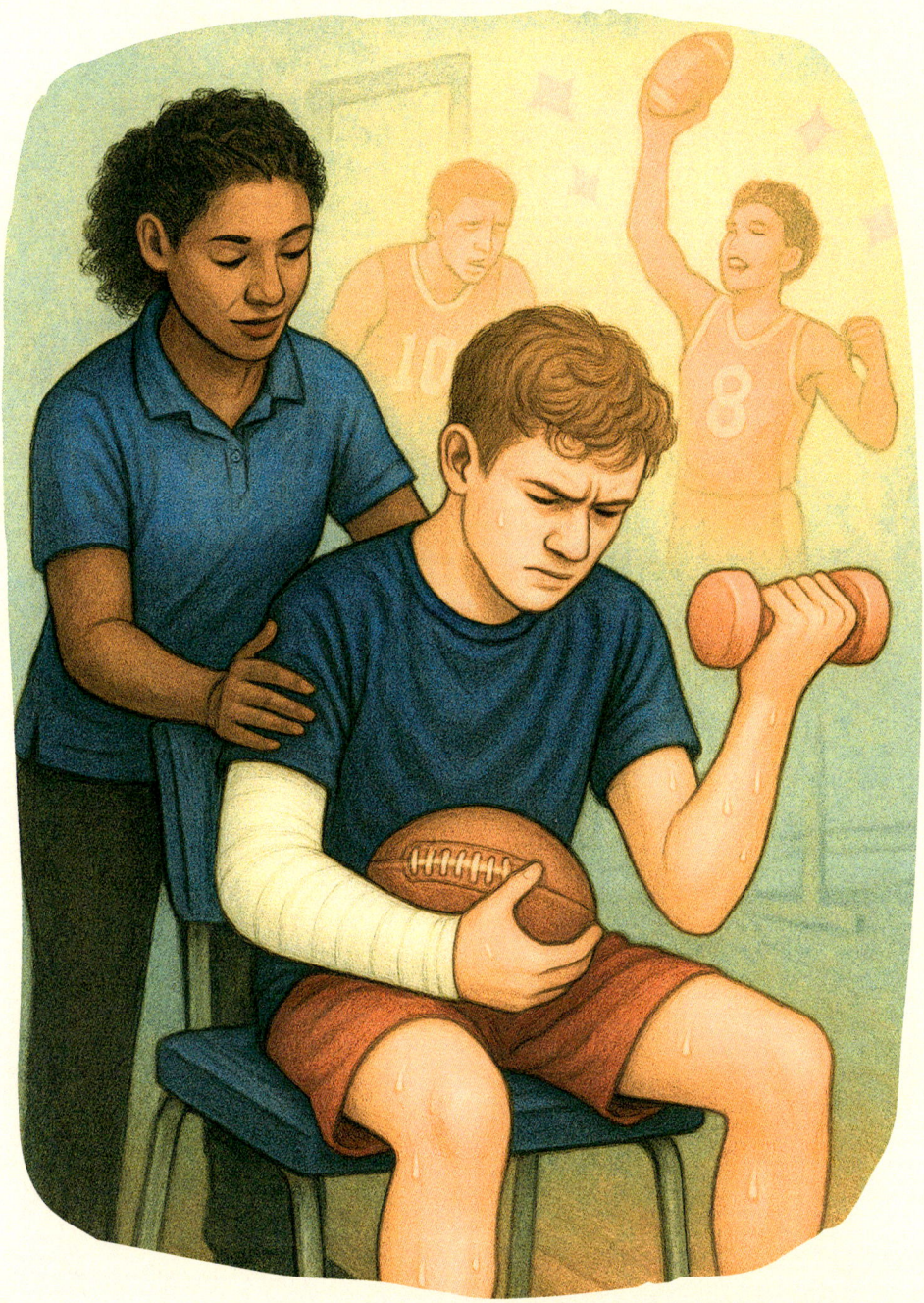

Journal Prompts

- What's a challenge you've faced that made you stronger?

- How do you react when things don't go as planned?

- What's one way you can build resilience in your life?

Challenge of the Week:

Reflect on a setback you've experienced and write down what you've learned from it.

Mindset Reminder:

"I am resilient. Every challenge is an opportunity for growth."

CHAPTER 17

Leadership

INSPIRING AND GUIDING OTHERS

"Leadership is not about being in charge. It's about taking care of those in your charge."

— Simon Sinek

Inspiring others and supporting them in their worst moments were things that came easy to Jake, especially in soccer. After every win, he would cheer on his teammates, leading the victory charge; likewise, he was always the first one to give an inspiring speech or anecdote in defeat to keep everyone else going. And though he wasn't the captain, Jake realized that leadership actually has nothing to do with your title. It's about uplifting those around you.

Leadership is about inspiring others to be their best. It's not about authority or control; it's about showing compassion, setting an example, and helping others succeed. You can be a leader in any situation by being thoughtful, proactive, and supportive.

Journal Prompts

- What qualities do you think make a good leader?

- Have you ever taken on a leadership role? How did it feel?

- Who in your life is a leader, and what do they teach you?

Challenge of the Week:

Find one opportunity to lead this week, whether it's helping a classmate, organizing a group project, or offering support.

Mindset Reminder:

"I am a leader, and I inspire others to be their best."

CHAPTER 18

Integrity
DOING WHAT'S RIGHT

"The time is always right to do what is right."
— *Martin Luther King Jr.*

Daniel wasn't a narc, but when he saw his friend cheating on a test he felt compelled to say something. It wasn't about being a rat or snitching on a friend – it was about doing the right thing. So, he told the teacher, and decided he would deal with the fallout later. To his surprise, his friend thanked him for being honest. Daniel learned that integrity isn't about avoiding hard choices; it's about doing the right thing, even when no one is watching.

Integrity is about being honest and doing the right thing, even when it's not easy. It's about aligning your actions with your values, whether you're alone or with others. Integrity builds trust and respect, both with yourself and those around you.

Journal Prompts

- What does integrity mean to you?

- Can you recall a time when you had to make a tough decision?

- How do you ensure your actions align with your values?

Challenge of the Week:

Think of one situation where you can practice integrity this week and follow through with it.

Mindset Reminder:

"I act with integrity. My actions reflect my values and strengthen my character."

CHAPTER 19

Balance

FINDING HARMONY IN LIFE

"Balance is not something you find, it's something you create."

— Jana Kingsford

Other kids at school had it easy: go to class, then go home. Emily's schedule was different. She was a diligent student, a promising athlete, and had a part-time job. It was a juggling act that she felt she had been failing. Her counselor suggested she take a step back and evaluate her priorities. Emily learned that balance wasn't about doing everything at once; it was about making time for what mattered most and finding moments of rest. By setting boundaries and managing her time better, Emily found more peace and focus in her life.

Balance is about finding harmony between your responsibilities, passions, and rest. When you try to do everything at once, you can burn out. Creating balance means taking care of your physical, mental, and emotional well-being, and knowing when to say no.

Journal Prompts

- How do you currently manage your time and energy?

- What activities help you feel balanced and centered?

- What can you do to improve the balance in your life?

Challenge of the Week:

Create a balanced schedule for your week, making sure to include time for work, rest, and activities you enjoy.

Mindset Reminder:

"I create balance in my life by prioritizing what matters most and taking care of myself."

CHAPTER 20

Humility
STAYING GROUNDED

"True humility is not thinking less of yourself; it is thinking of yourself less."

— C.S. Lewis

Isaiah wasn't one to shrug off the praise he received from others - he was an artist who was proud of his work, and enjoyed the admiration he received from others. When he met another artist whose work was arguably better than his, Isaiah was at first threatened, but quickly remembered to be humble. He set his ego aside, and rather than brush off the other artist, he admired their work, and the two shared their knowledge with one another.

Humility is about staying grounded, no matter how successful you become. It's about recognizing that everyone has something valuable to offer. Humility allows you to stay open to learning and growing, while also appreciating the talents and contributions of others.

Journal Prompts

- What does humility mean to you?

- When was the last time you learned something from someone else?

- How can you practice humility in your daily life?

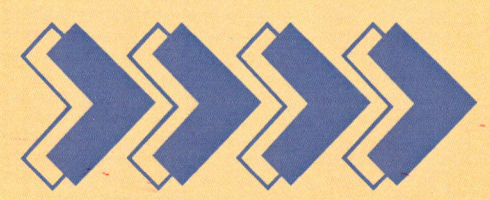

Challenge of the Week:

Find one way to recognize and appreciate someone else's strengths this week.

Mindset Reminder:

"I am humble and open to learning from others. We are all valuable."

CHAPTER 21

Change
EMBRACING GROWTH AND TRANSFORMATION

"The only way to make sense out of change is to plunge into it, move with it, and join the dance."

— Alan Watts

Olivia was used to her life back in her hometown, so when her family decided to move, the threat of change was scary. However, she quickly realized that with this change came new opportunities as well, and more room for growth. She was glad to have learned that lesson early in her life, that change is the one constant in the world, and the only one you can never predict. You have to move to the tempo.

Change can be unsettling, but it is also a powerful tool for growth. It's an opportunity to learn new things, face challenges, and discover new versions of yourself. When you embrace change with an open heart, you allow yourself to evolve and grow.

Journal Prompts

- How do you feel about change?

- Can you think of a time when change led to personal growth?

- How can you embrace change in your life?

Challenge of the Week:

Try something new or step out of your comfort zone this week to embrace change.

Mindset Reminder:

"Change is a part of life. I embrace it as an opportunity to grow and learn."

CHAPTER 22

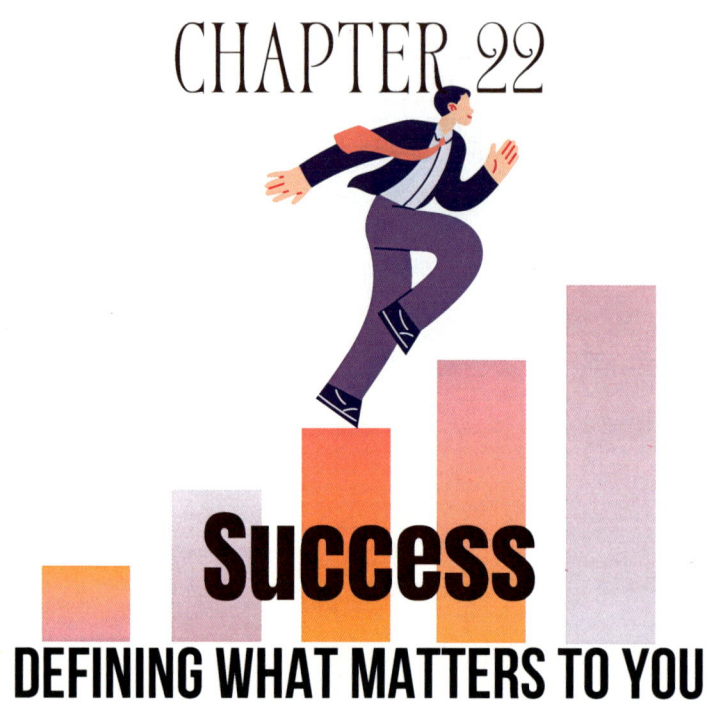

Success
DEFINING WHAT MATTERS TO YOU

"Success is not the key to happiness. Happiness is the key to success."

— Albert Schweitzer

All he wanted were the awards and recognition for the effort he put into his work, but when Lucas made it to the end of the year after non-stop grinding, he felt burnt out and unfulfilled. Something had to change. For Lucas, it meant redefining his goal posts: success would not be about awards, but about his own personal satisfaction. When he began to live his life according to his values, he felt much happier.

Success is different for everyone. It's not about comparing yourself to others, but about defining what brings you happiness and fulfillment. When you focus on what truly matters to you, you create a success story that is uniquely yours.

Journal Prompts

- What does success look like to you?

- How do you define happiness?

- What's one step you can take toward your personal definition of success?

Challenge of the Week:

Take time to define what success means to you and write down actionable steps to achieve it.

Mindset Reminder:

"Success is about living a life aligned with my values and finding fulfillment in every moment."

CHAPTER 23

Legacy
LEAVING A POSITIVE IMPACT

"The legacy you leave is the life you lead."

— *Unknown*

Sophia was determined to lead a good life, like her grandmother before her. She wanted money, fame, success, but when her grandmother passed away unexpectedly, Sophia realized that although her grandmother was indeed rich, famous, and successful, none of that would have meant anything if she wasn't a good person too. Sophia realized then that legacy was more than the wealth you accrue – it's about the lives you touch.

Your legacy is the impact you leave behind through your actions, kindness, and the relationships you build. It's not about fame or wealth, but about the positive influence you have on others. You have the power to leave a legacy that will inspire future generations.

Journal Prompts

- What kind of legacy do you want to leave?

- How do you want to be remembered by others?

- What small steps can you take now to create a positive impact?

Challenge of the Week:

Think of one way you can make a positive difference in someone's life this week.

CHAPTER 24

Prosperity
BUILDING SMART HABITS FOR FINANCIAL FREEDOM

"Don't just work for money; make your money work for you."
— Anonymous

Jayden got his first paycheck from a part-time job at a smoothie shop. He was ready to spend it all on new sneakers... Until his older cousin pulled him aside. "Before you blow it, think long term," she said, showing him how she tracked her spending, saved for college, and even started investing small amounts. Jayden didn't become a financial expert overnight, but he started budgeting. Saved 20%. Learned the difference between needs and wants.

A year later, he had enough to buy a laptop for his graphic design hustle without touching his savings. That's when he realized: smart money choices now = freedom later.

Money isn't just about spending, it's about choices. When you understand how money works, you gain power over your future. You don't have to be rich to build wealth. You just need to be wise. Budgeting, saving, investing, even knowing how to compare prices are small habits that lead to big freedom. Financial literacy is like learning a language: the earlier you start, the more fluent you become. And when you're financially free, you get to say yes to the life you actually want.

Journal Prompts

- What's something you've spent money on that brought real value?

- Where could you save or earn more if you got creative?

- What does "financial freedom" mean to you personally?

Challenge of the Week:

Track every dollar you spend for the next 7 days. At the end of the week, review it and find at least one area where you can spend smarter or save instead.

Mindset Reminder:

"I control my money, it doesn't control me."

ABOUT THE AUTHOR

Dr. Marlon Fuller is an entrepreneur, philanthropist, and inventor on a mission to help students level up in life. Alongside his wife Christina, he co-founded CoolKids.org, teaching over 30K students how to take charge of their futures and build financial confidence.

He's the mastermind behind JAR, the world's first streaming financial literacy TV app for kids, and The Syllabus, a series of G-rated financial literacy albums featuring celebrity collabs to make learning fun, relatable, and easy to understand.

Dr. Fuller also created FinLit Fest, the first-ever financial literacy music and business festival for middle and high school students. This annual event brings together experts, entrepreneurs, and celebrities to inspire and educate young people about money, entrepreneurship, and financial success.

His latest creation, Dear Future Me, is here to help students discover their passions, set meaningful goals, and grow with resilience. His mission? To give the next generation the tools to thrive and provide everything he wishes he knew growing up.

When he's not revolutionizing education, Dr. Fuller is traveling, giving back, and spending time with his wife and their four kids.

THE END

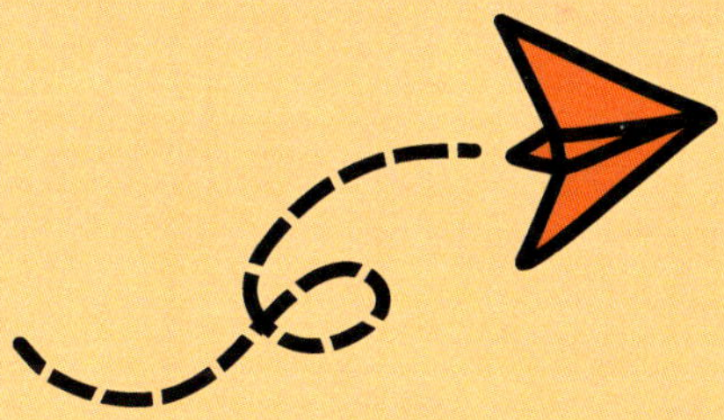

Made in United States
North Haven, CT
26 June 2025